Performance Management
A Practical Guide
Fourth Edition

Robert B. Maddux

A Crisp Fifty-Minute™ Series Book

This Fifty-Minute™ book is designed to be "read with a pencil." It is an excellent workbook for self-study as well as classroom learning. All material is copyright-protected and cannot be duplicated without permission from the publisher. *Therefore, be sure to order a copy for every training participant through our Web site, www.axzopress.com.*

Performance Management
A Practical Guide

Fourth Edition

Robert B. Maddux

CREDITS:
VP, Product Development: **Charlie Blum**
Production Editor: **Genevieve McDermott**
Production Artist: **Nicole Phillips**
Editor: **Carol Godding**
Copy Editor: **Charlotte Bosarge**
Cartoonist: **Ralph Mapson**

COPYRIGHT © 1986, 1987, 1993, 2000 Axzo Press. All Rights Reserved.

No part of this work may be reproduced, transcribed, or used in any form or by any means—graphic, electronic, or mechanical, including photocopying, recording, taping, Web distribution, or information storage and retrieval systems—without the prior written permission of the publisher.

Visit us online at **www.axzopress.com**

Trademarks
Crisp Fifty-Minute Series is a trademark of Axzo Press.

Some of the product names and company names used in this book have been used for identification purposes only and may be trademarks or registered trademarks of their respective manufacturers and sellers.

Disclaimer
We reserve the right to revise this publication and make changes from time to time in its content without notice.

ISBN 10: 1-4188-8914-8
ISBN 13: 978-1-4188-8914-2
Library of Congress Catalog Card Number 99-75-961
Printed in the United States

2 3 4 5 11 10 09

Learning Objectives For:

PERFORMANCE MANAGEMENT

The objectives for *Performance Management, Fourth Edition,* are listed below. They have been developed to guide the user to the core issues covered in this book.

THE OBJECTIVES OF THIS BOOK ARE TO HELP THE USER:

1) Understand principles of performance appraisals

2) Get tips for conducting an appraisal

3) Explore management leadership skills

ASSESSING PROGRESS

A Crisp Series **assessment** is available for this book. The 25-item, multiple-choice and true/false questionnaire allows the reader to evaluate his or her comprehension of the subject matter.

To download the assessment and answer key, go to www.axzopress.com and search on the book title.

Assessments should not be used in any employee selection process.

About the Author

Robert B. Maddux is president of Maddux Associates, Consultants in Human Resources Management. He has consulted extensively with large corporations and small businesses over the past twenty years to enable the mutually effective utilization of people in a variety of work environments. He has worked with many organizations and people in transition, and has been instrumental in facilitating the beginning of numerous new careers in business organizations and entrepreneurial ventures.

Mr. Maddux has designed and conducted management skills seminars in Canada, Europe, and throughout the United States, as well as consulted in the production of a number of management training films. He has written many Discussion Leader's Guides for use in employee development, and is the author of several best-selling management books.

Preface

This book is for anyone who directs the activities of others. Whether a first-line manager, the chairperson of a committee, a project leader, a school administrator, a government official, the owner of a small business, or a senior executive, you must be able to effectively discuss performance with those who report to you.

Leading a performance appraisal review can be either difficult and depressing, or dynamic and positive. The attitude, planning, and approach of the person conducting the review will make the difference.

This book will help you to think through the appraisal process, and then learn how to conduct discussions that encourage positive relationships and improve individual performance. Those who master the concepts presented will benefit from reduced stress and improved productivity.

You will have a chance to do some self-analysis, which will identify personal strengths and weaknesses. Once learned, the application of the skills is up to you.

Good luck!

Robert B. Maddux

Contents

Part 1: Are You Ready for Better Appraisals?
Objectives of Performance Appraisals 3
Meet Some Successes and Some Failures 4
Do You Put Off Performance Appraisals? 6
Benefits of a Well-Planned Appraisal 7
How Appraisals Help Employees 8

Part 2: Setting the Stage
Establish the Right Climate 13
Are You Part of the Solution or Part of the Problem? 14
Help Employees Find Meaning in Their Jobs and Stay on Course 19
Case Study 1: Who Will Be Better at Performance Appraisals? 21

Part 3: Preparing for More Effective Appraisals
What Is Meant by Goals and Standards? 25
Attitudes and Performance Appraisals 29
Employee Preparation for the Appraisal 34
Manager Preparation for the Appraisal 38
Pitfalls to Avoid 40
Elements of a Successful Appraisal 41
Develop an Action Plan 42
How Employee Performance Directs the Appraisal 43
Appraisal Discussion Models 44
Case Study 2: What Upset Jess? 46

Part 4: Conducting the Appraisal

Beginning the Appraisal Discussion 51
Discussing Unsatisfactory Performance 53
Getting an Employee to Talk Freely 54
Creating an Open Atmosphere 55
Appraisal Questions 57
Personal Development and Growth 61
The Importance of Attitude 62
Closing the Appraisal Discussion 66

Part 5: After the Appraisal

Following Up–Three Suggestions 71
Performance Appraisal Checklist for Managers 72
Creating a Personal Action Plan 75
Author's Suggested Answers to Cases 77

PART 1

Are You Ready for Better Appraisals?

Objectives of Performance Appraisal

Most managers want to succeed and to be effective in all aspects of their performance. However, frequent changes in assignments, organization, products, services, technology, skill and knowledge requirements, manufacturing processes, and delivery systems make this an ongoing challenge.

Employees face similar challenges. Whether they are organized along traditional lines or as teams, or function as individuals working alone, employees want to know what is expected of them personally, what's going on generally in the rest of the organization, how changes will affect their work, how they are doing, and how they can achieve their potential in their chosen field. Of course, questions should be answered when raised and performance errors corrected as they occur.

Periodic performance appraisal reviews can be designed to cover a wide range of topics or issues related to the organization, the manager, the employee, and how the work is performed. Employees and managers will want to cover all aspects of the employee's performance, development, and future prospects. Employees should also be given the opportunity at this time to give feedback on their view of their relationship with the manager and the organization and to share their aspirations in some detail. The performance appraisal objectives on the following pages are typical of many managers and employees.

A performance appraisal assures a periodic opportunity for communication between the person who assigns the work and the person who performs it, to discuss what they expect from each other and how well those expectations are being met. Performance appraisals are not adversary proceedings or social chitchat. They are an essential communication link between two people with a common purpose. Leading these discussions is not always easy, but the principles and techniques for effective sessions can be learned and applied by everyone. Some clues that will lead you toward success are included on the next page along with some pitfalls that lead to failure.

Meet Some Successes and Some Failures

Successes

➤ Leaders who establish clear, measurable expectations, and provide a climate conducive to success

➤ Leaders who engage in mutual goal-setting

➤ Leaders who ask questions, listen carefully, and appreciate the ideas of others

➤ Leaders who publicly recognize positive performance and privately correct improper performance when it occurs

➤ Leaders who look for the positives in every situation and seek constructive solutions to problems

➤ Leaders who follow through to ensure commitments are met

Add from your own experience: _____

_____

_____

_____

Failures

➤ Those who have not thought through what they expect or don't know how to measure success

➤ Those who establish arbitrary, unilateral performance goals or standards

➤ Those who rarely listen or seek ideas of others, yet have a solution for everyone else's problems

➤ Those who criticize performance openly in public or do not give credit where it is due

➤ Those who spend too much time looking for things that are wrong and too little time seeking those that are right

➤ Those who don't take their commitments seriously or don't know how to follow through

Add from your own experience: _____

_____

_____

_____

A good performance appraisal leaves both parties feeling they have gained something.

Do You Put Off Performance Appraisals?

The people who make things move in any situation are those with a sense of urgency about getting things done.

If you don't convey a sense of urgency in others, now is the time to start developing that skill. There are many competent people who are given good instructions but they never quite get things finished. Their achievements fall far short of those with less talent but a strong sense of "let's get it done now." The best way to pass a sense of urgency on to others is to show your personal interest in their work, check on progress, and provide constructive feedback.

Managers also need to develop a sense of urgency in getting performance appraisals done. Too often, performance appraisals are left until the last minute and then done in a hurried manner. When this occurs, the results are poor. The manager feels guilty, and the employee feels unimportant and let down.

> *"Time is the scarcest resource and unless it is managed, nothing else can be managed."*
>
> –Peter Drucker

Benefits of a Well-Planned Appraisal

People responsible for performance appraisals often assign a low priority to them because they have not thought about the benefits of a good appraisal session. Following are some advantages of doing a thoughtful appraisal on a timely basis. Check (✓) those that are important to you.

- ❑ Performance appraisals give me valuable insights into the work being done and those who are doing it.

- ❑ When I maintain good communication with others about job expectations and results, opportunities are created for new ideas and improved methods.

- ❑ Regular appraisal sessions remove surprises about how the quality of work is being perceived.

- ❑ When I do a good job appraising performance, anxiety is reduced because employees know how they are doing.

- ❑ I increase productivity when employees receive timely corrective feedback on their performance.

- ❑ I reinforce sound work practices and encourage good performance when I publicly recognize positive contributions.

- ❑ When I encourage two-way communication with employees, goals are clarified so they can be achieved or exceeded.

- ❑ When communication is two-way, I learn from others how I can improve as a manager.

- ❑ Learning to do professional performance appraisals is excellent preparation for advancement and increased responsibility.

How Appraisals Help Employees

Research reflects that more than half the professional and clerical employees working today do not understand how their work is evaluated. A survey recently completed by the Conference Board revealed that 60% of U.S. and European companies identified poor or insufficient performance feedback as a primary cause of deficient performance.

This research plus the frequently asked questions by employees, "Why didn't you tell me that's what you wanted in the first place?" or, "Why doesn't anyone ever tell me how I am doing?" leads one to believe employees need more thorough appraisals and a better understanding of the appraisal process. If this could be true of your employees, familiarize them with the process now and tell every new employee how they will be evaluated when they begin work.

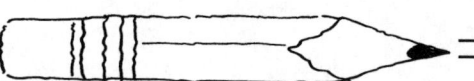

OPPORTUNITIES FOR PERFORMANCE APPRAISAL

Performance appraisal discussions are normally initiated by the manager, but are also appropriate when employees request a meeting to determine how well you think they are doing, to suggest changes in goals or standards, or to explore their needs for personal development. Check (✓) those that apply to you.

- ❏ **Appraisal discussions should be scheduled on a regular basis either by organizational policy or by the manager.**

- ❏ **Less formal discussions may be conducted whenever the nature of the assignment or other circumstances make it desirable to do so.**

- ❏ **An employee indicates the desire to discuss some aspects of his or her work or needs for personal growth.**

- ❏ **Leaders should provide praise for achievement whenever appropriate, and take prompt action to correct unsatisfactory performance when it occurs.**

- ❏ **Appraisal activities handled earlier at an appropriate time may be recalled later during a more formal, scheduled review for reinforcement.**

- ❏ **Follow-up discussions after a formal appraisal provide the opportunity for a broader review if needed.**

> *An entirely new system of thought is needed; a system based on attention to people, and not primarily attention to goods."*
>
> —E. F. Schumacher

10

PART 2

Setting the Stage

Establish the Right Climate

Performance appraisal has never been easy for managers or employees. Under the best of circumstances and in a reasonable business environment, performance appraisal requires sensitive attention to the needs of people, responsible concern for productivity, and open communication about the expectations of the organization. In an era of rapid change, the process becomes even more complex.

Warren Bennis, co-author of *Leaders*, was asked following a speech to describe the current management scene. He said, "It is the most difficult, treacherous, blind time in history." No one in his audience disagreed.

Modern managers have been caught in a whirlpool of change that has often diminished their financial resources, reduced their staff, cut their training budget, and increased their personal workload. They have witnessed, and often presided over, the elimination of layers of management and support staff that included many friends and trusted associates.

Conditions at home, in the community, and throughout the world are also changing rapidly. Working couples and single parents are stressed by the need for child and elder care, the pursuit of careers, conflicting goals, and changing roles in the home. On the national front, major concerns include a deteriorating educational system, the national debt, poverty, crime, substance abuse, and continuing issues pertaining to religion, race, and sexual preference. People are overwhelmed by the complexity of the problems and long for both answers and anchors in their life at home and at work.

Organizations, while contributing to some of these complexities, need their managers and employees to focus fully on productivity, profitability, and customer satisfaction to be successful in a global economy. Managers, as always, are expected to balance the needs of individuals and the company.

> *The art of progress is to preserve order amid change and to preserve change amid order.*
>
> —**Alfred North Whitehead**

Are You Part of the Solution or Part of the Problem?

> *Streamlined bureaucracies may translate into higher profits, more responsive customer service and faster product development, but they are also forcing difficult adjustments in how managers work. Many managers must adapt to fuzzier lines of authority and greater emphasis on teamwork.*
>
> *Low level managers, accustomed to carrying out orders, suddenly are asked to set strategy. For most, a leaner structure means not only increased workloads, but also diminished chances for promotion, and the frustration that fosters."*
>
> –Carol Hymowitz

To set a climate for effective performance appraisals today, the manager has to work harder than ever before to provide a working environment in which employees can find definitions of their work, the organization's goals, a future they can believe in, and meaning for their own career. Before managers can help establish this environment for employees, however, they must first do it for themselves.

 **Managers who are not committed to the goals of their organization will not be helpful to employees or effective appraisers of performance.**

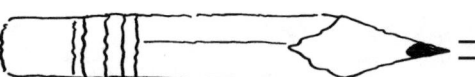

TEST YOUR REALITIES

Whether or not you have experienced major change in your organization and assignment, it pays to ask yourself periodically, "Why am I here? What am I supposed to do? How well am I doing it?" In the list below, check (✓) your current realities.

- ❏ 1. I am busier than ever before.
- ❏ 2. My vision of the future is fuzzy and I am not sure where to focus.
- ❏ 3. Employees are upset, confused, and demoralized.
- ❏ 4. Expectations of me exceed my ability to produce.
- ❏ 5. I am understaffed.
- ❏ 6. I have to delegate to people whom I feel are not ready.
- ❏ 7. Resources to reward good work are very limited.
- ❏ 8. Employees spend more time worrying than working.
- ❏ 9. I don't know how much longer my job will last.
- ❏ 10. The organization's actions are increasingly difficult to support.
- ❏ 11. My relationships with people are growing weaker.
- ❏ 12. I never felt better in my life.
- ❏ 13. I know exactly where the organization is going.
- ❏ 14. Organization priorities are clear to me.
- ❏ 15. Expectations of employees are easy to define.
- ❏ 16. It is easy to keep employees focused.
- ❏ 17. Leading and motivating employees is not a problem.
- ❏ 18. Career opportunities for employees are plentiful.
- ❏ 19. Advancement opportunities for me are evident.
- ❏ 20. Morale continues to improve.
- ❏ 21. Resources are available to properly reward good work.
- ❏ 22. Performance appraisal usually goes smoothly.

If you checked any of the first eleven items, it is strongly suggested you do some serious analysis of your current realities and the climate for performance appraisal in your organization. The following pages should be helpful.

Get Your Act Together

Managers who are uncertain about an organization's vision of the future, and are tentative in terms of their own personal commitment to what they perceive as its primary goals, will not do an adequate job themselves (much less, favorably influence the work of others). Regardless of how this condition comes about, there are two basic ways to take corrective action. One is to get your act together and the other is to leave the organization. Those who wish to first try getting their act together will find the following suggestions helpful.

1. If you are in an organization in transition, it will help you to clarify issues if you list what you have lost, what has stayed the same, and what you have gained.

   Lost : _____

   _____

   _____

   Stayed the same: _____

   _____

   _____

   Gained: _____

   _____

   _____

2. Identify exactly what it is that is bothering you. (Summarize below or take a sheet of paper and write it out in detail.)

   _____

   _____

   _____

   _____

3. List the issues, obstacles, or people preventing you from making a strong commitment, establishing goals, and developing expectations with your employees:

   Issues: _____

   _____

   _____

   Obstacles: _____

   _____

   _____

   People: _____

   _____

   _____

4. Describe your attitude and its likely impact on others with whom you work: _____

   _____

   _____

5. Share your concerns with persons who can do something about them. List their names below: _____

   _____

   _____

   _____

   _____

GET YOUR ACT TOGETHER (CONT)

6. Identify the contributions your unit can make to the organization:

   _____
   _____
   _____
   _____

7. List six actions you will take to help your group make the contributions you have identified:

   1. _____
   2. _____
   3. _____
   4. _____
   5. _____
   6. _____

> "*A rock pile ceases to be a rock pile the moment a single man contemplates it, bearing within him the image of a cathedral.*"
>
> –Antoine de Saint-Exupery

Help Employees Find Meaning in Their Jobs and Stay on Course

> *"Example is not the main thing in influencing others. It's the only thing."*
>
> —Albert Schweitzer

If you sometimes find it difficult to understand and commit to the current and future needs of your organization, isn't it likely your employees have similar problems? Doesn't it seem logical that they need your leadership to help them understand the issues and focus effort in the right places? When you have your act together, you can help employees do the same. Your efforts, and theirs, will create a climate in which performance appraisal is meaningful and mutually supportive. Here are some tips on how to make it happen successfully. Check (✓) those you are now using or will use in the future.

- ❑ Reflect a positive "can and will do" attitude.

- ❑ Demonstrate personal flexibility and adaptability.

- ❑ Communicate your vision of the future and how it is bridged to the present.

- ❑ Identify and talk through the concerns of each individual.

- ❑ Discuss and clarify organizational, personal, and employee objectives. Reduce ambiguity.

- ❑ Help employees assess their current role, express your expectations, and develop a plan to meet job requirements together.

- ❑ Determine what employees consider to be problems and involve them in finding solutions.

- ❑ Quickly fix those things that are broken.

Help Employees Find Meaning in Their Jobs and Stay on Course (CONT)

- ❏ Show employees the importance of letting go of the past, focusing on the present, and anticipating change in the future.

- ❏ Help employees determine how their personal career goals can be achieved or made more realistic.

- ❏ Encourage employees to show some initiative and to risk a little. They will grow in the process.

- ❏ Use delegation to educate and develop people.

- ❏ Be creative in finding ways to recognize and reward desired performance.

- ❏ Recognize genuine attempts to achieve as well as the achievements themselves.

- ❏ Make sure policies and procedures always support and never prevent the accomplishment of objectives.

- ❏ Ask your employees frequently what you and/or the organization are doing that makes them uncomfortable and inhibits their performance.

- ❏ Be sure your behavior and communication practices continue to be consistent and congruent with what you expect from others.

- ❏ If your organization is in transition, discuss the emotional impacts with employees so they will understand what they are experiencing is normal. Help them move on to a new commitment as soon as possible.

Performance appraisal should make every employee aware of the importance of the contribution they are expected to make.

Case Studies

The case studies that appear throughout this book, beginning with the one on this page, present issues and problems that occur in the work setting, then ask you to provide an answer or solution. These cases are designed to provide insights about the context that has been, or is about to be, presented. Completing each study as you proceed will help you reality-test the material and retain the information.

The first case should help you understand some of the groundwork necessary to complete a successful performance appraisal and discussion.

Always compare your answers with those of the author (given at the back of the book). In addition, you may wish to discuss the case with other managers to take advantage of their experience and expertise.

CASE STUDY 1

Who Will Be Better at Performance Appraisals?

Janice and Arminio are new managers attending their first training workshop. They have not covered material on performance appraisals yet, but are discussing their philosophies about them over lunch. Janice doesn't believe a fair performance appraisal can be made of an employee's work unless assignments have been discussed, and expectations agreed upon in advance. She thinks work should be assigned in measurable terms so both she and employee can track performance as the work progresses.

Arminio thinks this approach is dangerous. He thinks employees should be given only a general idea of what is to be accomplished. He thinks employees who participate in establishing performance objectives will set their goals too low. He prefers to leave performance expectations vague to see what the employees accomplish on their own. If their standards don't measure up, he will let them know then and there.

Your Turn

Who do you think will be the best at performance appraisals?

        Janice ❑   Arminio ❑

Because: _____

_____

_____

_____

_____

_____

Turn to the back of the book for the author's views.

PART 3

Preparing for More Effective Appraisals

What Is Meant by Goals and Standards?

The appraisal process starts when the employee and manager reach a mutual understanding of what needs to be accomplished. If expectations are not clearly stated, mutually understood, and presented in measurable terms, performance will be difficult to evaluate.

Goals and standards are methods by which job expectations can be expressed. Those responsible for performance appraisals need a good understanding of goals and standards, and how to use them during the appraisal process.

Goals

A goal is a statement of results to be achieved. Goals describe:

➤ conditions that will exist when the desired outcome has been accomplished

➤ a time frame during which the outcome is to be completed

➤ resources the organization is willing to commit to achieve the desired result

Goals should be challenging but achievable. Goals should be established with the participation of those responsible for meeting them. Here is an example:

> *"To increase the flow of invoices through the Accounting Department to a minimum of 150 per day by October 1. The total cost increase to accomplish this should not exceed $550."*

Once accomplished, a new goal can be established to emphasize the next set of desired results.

Standards

A standard refers to ongoing performance criteria that must be met time and time again. Standards are usually expressed quantitatively, and refer to such things as attendance, breakage, manufacturing tolerances, production rates, and safety standards. Like goals, they are most effective when established with the participation of those who must meet them. Here is an example:

> *"The departmental filing backlog should not exceed one week. Any record requested should be available within five minutes of the request."*

In general, goals apply more to managers and professional employees who engage in individualized projects. Standards are more common for workers engaged in routine, repetitive tasks.

When employees participate in setting goals and standards, there should be no mystery about how their performance will be judged. Employees cannot say, "Why didn't you tell me that's what you wanted?" or, "Who dreamed up these impossible standards?"

Since goals and/or standards are the primary criteria by which performance will be measured, it is worth reviewing them. Please complete the exercise on the facing page.

For more information on effective goal setting, refer to <u>Partners in Performance</u>, *Crisp Series.*

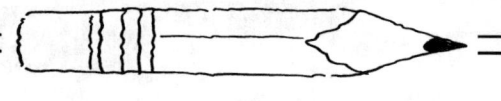

IDENTIFY GOALS AND STANDARDS

For the following list of statements, write a "**G**" in the space provided if it is a goal and an "**S**" if it is a standard. If the statement is neither a goal nor a standard, leave the space blank. Answers are on the following page.

_____ 1. Breakage in the kitchen should be kept to a minimum.

_____ 2. To eliminate maintenance coding errors for existing computer programs by October 1, at a cost not to exceed 40 work hours.

_____ 3. Reduce the cost of ongoing operations by January 1.

_____ 4. Telephones are to be answered quickly and messages taken when necessary.

_____ 5. To reduce burner maintenance expense by 15% before November 15, at a onetime cost not to exceed $10,000.

_____ 6. To increase sales of men's watches by 10% before June 1, with no increase in expense.

_____ 7. Appreciably reduce lost time because of accidents by year-end.

_____ 8. Errors in recording class enrollment will not exceed 2% of the total monthly enrollment.

_____ 9. Telephones should be answered after no more than two rings. Telephone manners are expected to follow those prescribed in the company handbook. Messages should include date, time of call, relevant names and numbers, and the nature of the call.

_____ 10. To increase Western Region sales by $200,000 by year-end at an increased cost of sales of less than 5%.

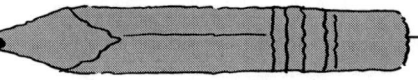

ANSWERS

Items 2, 5, 6, and 10 are measurable goals (**G**).

Items 8 and 9 are measurable standards (**S**).

Items 1, 3, 4, and 7 are neither goals nor standards.

Our attitude toward people determines our approach to performance appraisals. Some managers perform performance appraisals well because their attitude toward people sets them on a positive course. Others are less successful because their attitude creates a negative climate. The next page describes three different attitudes. Which one best describes you?

Attitudes and Performance Appraisals

> *"Make it thy business to know thyself, which is the most difficult lesson in the world."*
>
> —Miguel de Cervantes

Check (✓) the one that best describes you.

- ❏ **"I know best."**

    This person feels work should be done by controlling the people who do it. Employees are told what to do, how to do it, and when to stop. Then they are told what they did wrong and what they did right, where they are weak, and where they are strong. The person in charge feels this is justified because of his or her superior knowledge and ability. This attitude does not invite new ideas or challenge people. Communication is directed one way only.

- ❏ **"I'll set the goals; you meet them."**

    This person feels that because of superior knowledge, ability, or experience, it is OK to set goals for others to meet. The employee is given an opportunity to discuss ways to meet goals, but has no input into the actual performance objectives. Performance is evaluated on how well original goals were achieved, regardless of how realistic they were.

- ❏ **"Let's review the work together, establish some realistic goals, and evaluate performance accordingly."**

    This person emphasizes work performance, not worker characteristics. The idea is to help workers evaluate the usefulness of their ideas, recognize their weaknesses, and exploit their strengths. The manager acts as a resource and enabler, rather than as a judge.

Personal characteristics and experience influence how you do as an appraiser. Now is a good time to evaluate your personal skills and to give some serious thought to how you can improve. Complete the personal assessment on the facing page as objectively as you can, and it will give you some very good ideas about where to begin. Then make a commitment to improve your skills in any area indicated by your ratings.

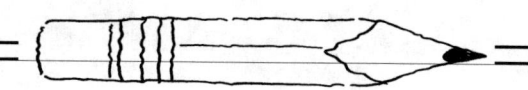

Are You an Effective Appraiser?

The following personal characteristics support effective performance appraisals. This scale will help identify your strengths, and determine areas where improvement would be beneficial. Circle the number that best reflects where you fall on the scale; the higher the number, the more the characteristic describes you. When you have finished, total the numbers circled in the space provided below.

1. I like being responsible for productivity.
   10   9   8   7   6   5   4   3   2   1

2. I like people and enjoy talking with them.
   10   9   8   7   6   5   4   3   2   1

3. I don't mind giving criticism of a constructive nature.
   10   9   8   7   6   5   4   3   2   1

4. I give praise freely when is earned.
   10   9   8   7   6   5   4   3   2   1

5. I am not intimidated by workers who tell me what they really think.
   10   9   8   7   6   5   4   3   2   1

6. I seek new ideas and use them whenever possible.
   10   9   8   7   6   5   4   3   2   1

7. I respect the knowledge and skill of the people who work for me.
   10   9   8   7   6   5   4   3   2   1

8. I follow up to be sure commitments, goals, and standards are being met.
   10   9   8   7   6   5   4   3   2   1

9. I am sensitive to the needs and feelings of others.
   10   9   8   7   6   5   4   3   2   1

10. I am not worried by employees who know more about their work than I do.
    10   9   8   7   6   5   4   3   2   1

TOTAL _____

WHERE ARE YOU?

A score between 90 and 100 indicates you have excellent characteristics to conduct effective appraisals. A score between 70 and 89 indicates that you have significant strengths, but also some improvement needs. Scores between 50 and 69 reflect a significant number of problem areas. Scores below 50 call for a serious effort to improve. Make a special effort to grow in any area where you scored 6 or less, regardless of your total score.

Leading a performance appraisal discussion can be compared to baseball

➤ Every session requires a team effort and a game plan.

➤ Winning depends on how well the team has prepared.

➤ Each player needs a turn at bat.

➤ Four basic essentials (bases) need to be covered in each meeting to achieve maximum results.

You make it to second base when both parties freely communicate key aspects of job performance.

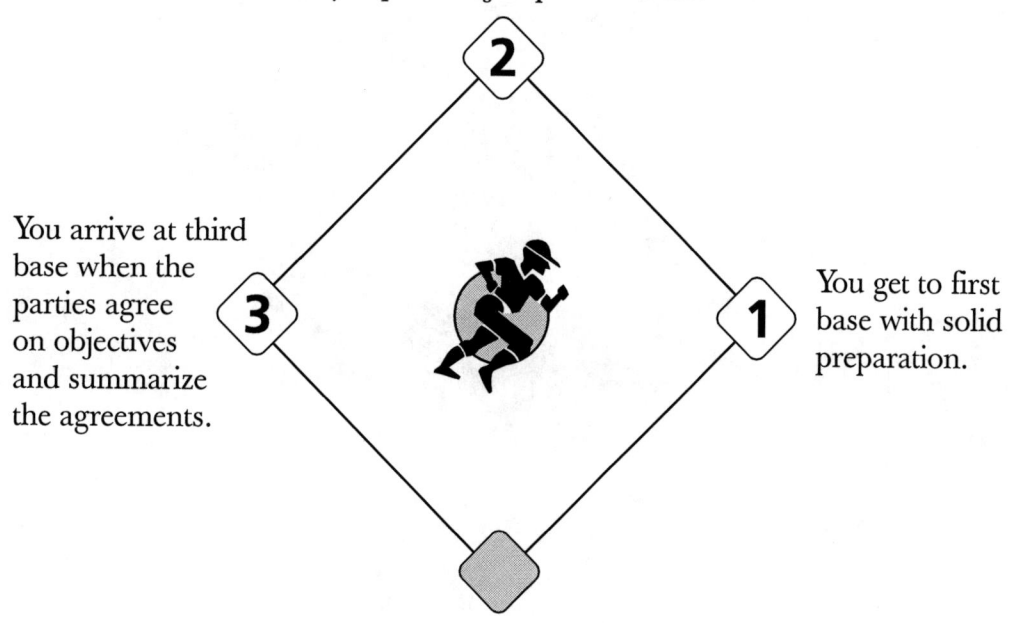

You arrive at third base when the parties agree on objectives and summarize the agreements.

You get to first base with solid preparation.

You score a home run when post-appraisal follow-up reflects a job well done by both parties.

Cover All the Bases

Employee Preparation for the Appraisal

The appraisal discussion is a structured and planned interpersonal meeting, not a casual conversation. Preparation for the appraisal discussion is, therefore, as important to the employee as it is to the manager.

Employees should be well informed about the purpose of the appraisal, the process, and how the results will be used. Emphasis on the need for two-way communication will encourage the employee to share his or her insights so they can be factored into the outcome.

It is also helpful to highlight topics for discussion and set a specific time, agreeable to both parties, in advance so both can prepare accordingly.

Help employees prepare by providing them with an advance copy of "Thought Stimulators for Self-Appraisal," printed on the next page.

THOUGHT STIMULATORS FOR SELF-APPRAISAL

These questions can help you prepare for your performance appraisal. As you read each question, think about your performance, your progress, and your plans for future growth.

1. What critical abilities does my job require? To what extent do I fulfill them? _____
   _____

2. What do I like best about my job? _____
   _____
   Least? _____

3. What were my specific accomplishments during this appraisal period? _____
   _____

4. Which goals or standards did I fall short of meeting? _____
   _____
   _____

5. How could my manager help me do a better job? _____
   _____

6. Is there anything that the organization or my manager does to hinder my effectiveness? _____
   _____

THOUGHT STIMULATORS FOR SELF-APPRAISAL (CONT)

7. What changes would improve my performance? _____
_____

8. Does my present job make the best use of my capabilities? How could I become more productive? _____
_____

9. What do I expect to be doing five years from now? _____
_____

10. Do I need more experience or training in any aspect of my current job? How could it be accomplished? _____
_____

11. What have I done since my last appraisal to prepare myself for more responsibility? _____
_____

12. What new goals and standards should be established for the next appraisal period? Which old ones need to be modified or deleted?
_____
_____

You have permission to copy this self-appraisal for your employees.

How to Get to First Base

Preparation! Preparation! Preparation!

When a performance appraisal goes poorly, it is usually because the manager has not prepared properly or completely, or has not given the employee the opportunity to prepare.

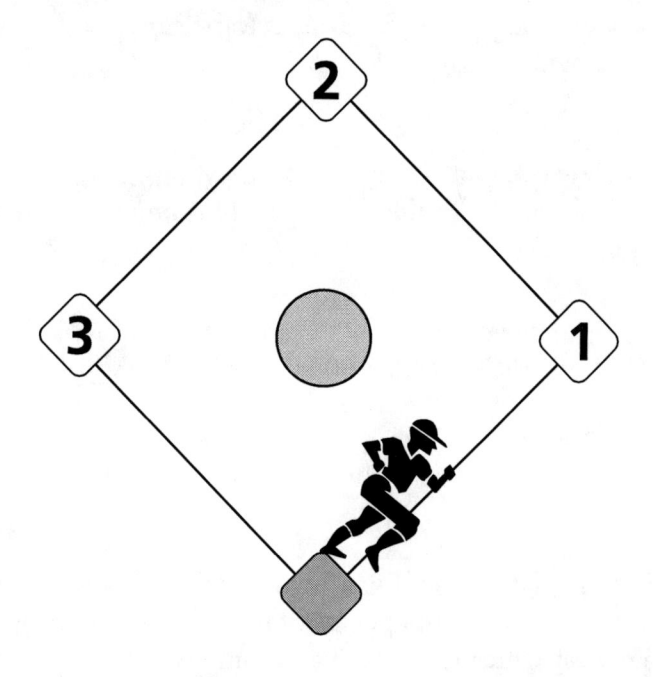

Manager Preparation for the Appraisal

Prior to conducting a performance appraisal, identify and develop items to be covered. Since employee performance in the current job is the central issue, gather relevant data concerning job requirements and the established goals or standards. Next, assess the employee's performance on the above for the appraisal period. Then:

1 **Review the job requirements** to be sure you fully understand them.

2 **Review the goals and standards** you previously discussed and agreed upon with the employee (plus any notes you have relating to their achievement).

3 **Review the employee's history**, including:
- job skills
- training
- past jobs and job performance

4 **Identify any special assignments** the employee has worked on during the appraisal period, whether under your jurisdiction or not. What specifically was to be accomplished? Were expectations met? What was the employee's contribution to the final outcome?

5 **Review the employee's team performance**, whether in a permanent assignment or a one-shot project. Performance measures can be derived from the team's expected deliverables. If the team involved is cross-functional, the performance of each member can be measured by his or her personal contributions to the final result. Also consider the team's self-appraisal, if available.

6 **Seek input from customers** with whom the employee has direct and frequent contact. "Customers" may include anyone who utilizes products or services from your unit or department.

7 **Evaluate job performance** versus job expectations for the period being appraised, and rate it from unacceptable to outstanding.

8 **Note any variances** in the employee's performance that need to be discussed. Provide specific examples.

9 **Consider career opportunities** or limitations for this person. Be prepared to discuss them.

Pitfalls to Avoid

Factors that mislead or blind us when we are in the appraisal process are pitfalls to be avoided. An appraiser must be on guard against anything that distorts reality, favorably or unfavorably. Some typical pitfalls include:

- **Bias/Prejudice:** things we tend to react to that have nothing to do with performance such as race, religion, education, family background, age, and/or gender

- **Trait Assessment:** too much attention to characteristics that have nothing to do with the job and are difficult to measure. Examples include characteristics such as flexibility, sincerity, or friendliness.

- **Over-emphasis on favorable or unfavorable performance of one or two tasks:** could lead to an unbalanced evaluation of the overall condition

- **Relying on impressions rather than facts**

- **Holding the employee responsible for the impact of factors beyond his or her control**

- **Failure to provide each employee with an opportunity for advance preparation**

> **TIP:** Concentrate on performance measured against mutually-understood expectations.

Elements of a Successful Appraisal

In an appraisal discussion, five fundamental areas need to be covered:

1 **The measurement of results of the employee's performance against goals and standards**

2 **Recognition of the employee's contributions**

3 **Correction of any new or ongoing performance problems**

4 **Training and personal development needs for both current and future applications**

5 **The establishment of goals and/or standards for the next appraisal period**

Everything of substance during the discussion should relate to these elements, and both parties should actively participate in the discussion. An action plan prepared in advance will help keep the discussion on target.

Develop an Action Plan

Once you have completed your planning review, you will need to develop an action plan for the appraisal. Keep the following guidelines in mind.

- Don't cover too many areas in any one discussion. Concentrate on those that deserve the most attention.

- Make sure there are specific, unbiased examples that can be used to support your points but that also allow for dialogue.

- Develop positive approaches to correcting problems. Give the employee an opportunity to suggest solutions before any final decisions are made.

- Be prepared to provide praise and positive reinforcement for items that deserve it.

- Identify developmental activities that will improve the employee's performance in the present assignment, and/or provide preparation for future assignments.

- Note any projects, goals, and/or standards to be accomplished during the forthcoming appraisal period. Discuss them and reach agreement on them during the session.

- Plan to involve the employee in all aspects of the discussion.

How Employee Performance Directs the Appraisal

Outstanding? Unsatisfactory? Satisfactory?

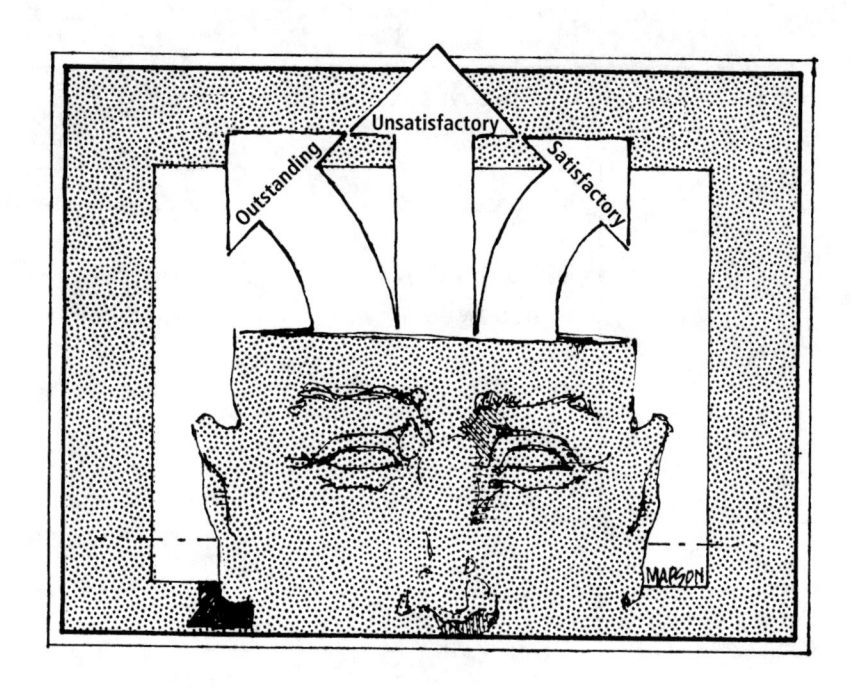

Your conclusions from the evaluation should be your primary guide in structuring the appraisal discussion. The employee's performance, for example, may suggest improving knowledge and skill sets to strengthen performance in the current assignment. On the other hand, it may suggest the timing is ideal for discussing the employee's aspirations and needs for future growth. It could be the time to let the employee know that his or her performance must improve or he or she will be terminated. You must decide and plan the substance of your discussion accordingly.

Read on for some suggested approaches. Have your discussion objectives well in mind as you prepare.

Appraisal Discussion Models

Your overall evaluation of an employee will range from outstanding to unsatisfactory. Select an approach to your appraisal discussion that is in keeping with your evaluation. The employee, for example, may be outstanding in the current assignment, but unpromotable because certain key skills are lacking. You have to decide how to handle each case. Following are some possible discussion models.

End result of evaluation	Employee's likely future	Discussion objective
OUTSTANDING	Promotion	Consider opportunities
	Growth in present assignment	Make development plans
	Broadened assignment	Review possibility of extending responsibility
	No change in duties	How to maintain performance level
SATISFACTORY	Promotion	Consider possibilities
	Growth in present assignment	Make development plans
	No change in duties	How to maintain or improve performance level
UNSATISFACTORY	Performance correctable	Plan correction and gain commitment
	Performance uncorrectable	Review possible re-assignment, or prepare for termination

> *"All labor that uplifts humanity has dignity and importance and should be undertaken with painstaking excellence."*
>
> —Dr. Martin Luther King Jr.

Managers are usually quick to take action when they have problems with such things as system failures, machine overloads, mechanical breakdowns, and the loss of customer confidence. In fact, they often have backup systems ready to take over at the first sign of a malfunction, as well as preventative maintenance programs to reduce the risk of an interruption in the flow of goods and services.

Unfortunately, too many managers do not have the same concern for the performance of people as they do for their systems and machines. They do not realize that people need periodic maintenance too, and their productivity suffers when they are not given at least the same consideration as hardware. Dialogue and the exchange of feedback at the appropriate time often fulfill the needs of both the employee and the manager—unless, of course, it is handled in a manner similar to that presented in Case Study 2 on the following page.

Now is a good time to apply what you have read so far. Analyze the case on the basis of what you have learned.

CASE STUDY 2

What Upset Jess?

Darcy just completed a performance appraisal discussion with one of her employees and is upset about it. She told another manager at lunch, "I appraised Jess this morning. I had to call him out of the budget meeting because I remembered all my appraisals were due today. I couldn't believe his reaction. He said he had no time to prepare, and expected me to have an example to support each criticism I made. About all he did, really, was to criticize my position on a couple of issues. I told him several things I didn't like about his performance, and then was good enough to tell him how to correct his faults. All I got back was anger and silence! You would think he would be grateful for some feedback, but I guess people today don't really care about improving. Normally he's a pretty good employee, but he was sure upset during the appraisal. What do you suppose is wrong with him anyway?"

Your Turn

Please use the space below to write down what you think is "wrong" with Jess.

_____
_____
_____
_____
_____
_____
_____
_____
_____
_____
_____

Compare your response with the author's in the back of the book.

PART 4

Conducting the Appraisal

50

Beginning the Appraisal Discussion

Managers have the responsibility to initiate appraisal discussions. Although individual personalities influence the tone and format, experts agree the discussion should be held in a private place to avoid interruptions and should begin on a positive and friendly note. While chitchat will help break the ice, both parties will welcome getting down to business.

One way to accomplish this is to highlight a specific positive achievement and discuss it first. Another approach is to ask the employee to review his or her accomplishments for the appraisal period. This allows the employee to select where to begin and can lead to a candid assessment of actual performance. While the employee is talking, the manager should be an interested listener.

If variances between expectations and results are evident, it is important both manager and employee try to determine what they are and why they occurred. This helps the discussion become a joint problem-solving session that can lead to the implementation of effective solutions.

The employee should be encouraged to identify as many reasons for variances as possible. None should be rejected right away, even if they seem to be excuses. The manager should also suggest possible causes so nothing significant is overlooked. This sharing allows for an exchange of viewpoints. This can provide better insights for all concerned and lead to a new understanding of the expectations of the organization, and the people who staff it.

> **TIP** Successful discussion leaders believe employees should do most of the talking. This can be achieved by using good communication skills and an atmosphere that encourages discussion.

Getting to Second Base

You make it to second base when both the manager and the employee communicate about all aspects of the job. It's not as easy as it sounds!

Experts believe that at least 50% of performance problems in business occur because of a lack of feedback. An employee sees no reason to change performance if it appears acceptable to the manager and the organization.

The next page includes some ways to approach constructive feedback, and maintain a climate conducive to a win/win outcome.

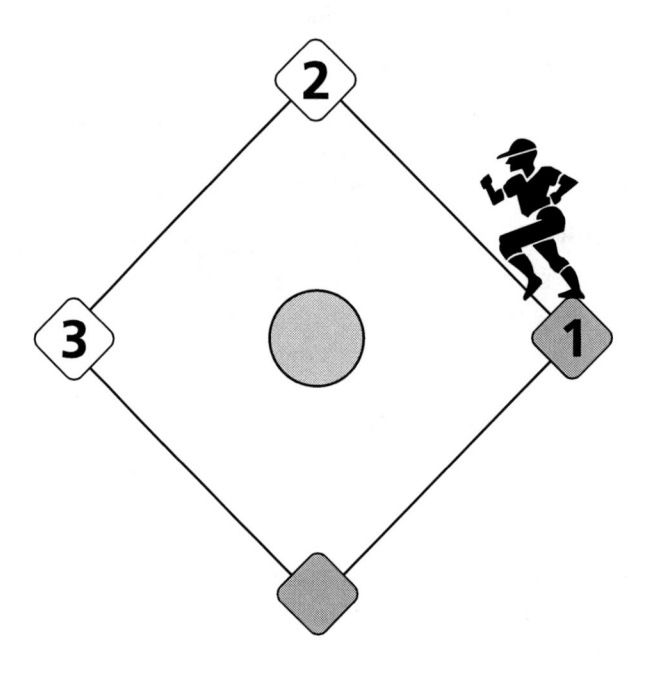

Never Ignore Unsatisfactory Performance

Discussing Unsatisfactory Performance

Employees who work in a nonthreatening atmosphere are more likely to discuss their shortcomings in the appraisal setting. When this occurs, the manager can be supportive by saying something like, "That's very perceptive. What can we do to correct this situation?"

If the employee has been unsatisfactory in an aspect of his or her job, and does not bring up areas of weak performance, the manager must do so. It helps to be able to describe the impact of the poor performance on the organization.

Some employees may not realize they are falling short of expectations. Or they may assume everything is acceptable because no one has ever discussed the problem with them. Sometimes they may feel everything is OK because they see others doing the same thing.

A first step to correct unsatisfactory performance is to review expectations. If the employee is unaware of these expectations, they must be made clear, and a commitment made that they will be met. If expectations are not being met for some other reason, the manager must first learn why, and then agree on a corrective action plan worked out with the employee.

Questions like these can be helpful in opening up issues:

- "Are you aware of the standards for quantity and quality we expect on this item?"

- "Are you aware of your error rate versus the departmental average?"

- "We seem to be running about two weeks behind schedule; can you tell me why, and what we can do to catch up?"

- "Your sales reports are excellent but they are never on time. Can you explain why?"

- "50% of your staff resigned in the last quarter. To what do you attribute that?"

Getting an Employee to Talk Freely

Employees often say very little during an appraisal discussion. There are several possible reasons for this. Some include:

- ❏ The employee does not understand the purpose of the appraisal, and is afraid to express an opinion.

- ❏ The employee is not given the opportunity to express an opinion.

- ❏ The employee was not given time to prepare for the discussion.

- ❏ The employee's thoughts and ideas are quickly brushed aside or discounted.

- ❏ The employee is experiencing a significant personal crisis, e.g., serious illness or death in the family, which is affecting performance.

- ❏ The employee is angry.

- ❏ The employee feels the whole process is meaningless.

! TIP   Managers learn more from listening than talking!

For more information on how to build skills in this area, refer to <u>Coaching and Counseling</u>, *and* <u>Handling the Difficult Employee</u>, *Crisp Series.*

Creating an Open Atmosphere

Check (✓) those methods you expect to use.

❏ 1. Be descriptive rather than judgmental.

When a manager is judgmental about an employee's performance, it almost always brings out defensive behavior in the employee. A better climate is established when descriptive terms are used to address problems. This makes it possible for the manager and employee to unemotionally discuss a solution, or, even better, a solution generated by the employee. Note the differences in the following examples:

> **Judgmental:** "How could you do such a dumb thing?"

> **Descriptive:** "Can you explain what caused the incident?"

Managers who use descriptive, nonjudgmental language in the appraisal discussion show a desire to analyze and resolve a problem, not find a scapegoat or way to demean the employee.

❏ 2. Be supportive, not authoritarian.

Managers sometimes purposely, and sometimes inadvertently, display an authoritarian attitude during the discussion. This can create resentment and defensiveness. It is usually better to respect the employee's ability to contribute to the solution of a problem. Here is an example:

> **Authoritarian:** "Here is what we will do to get this done on time."

> **Supportive:** "What do you suggest we do to get this done on time in the future?"

Supportive practices generate options for problem-solving because the employee is encouraged to make suggestions. They focus on the problem, not the employee. In addition, a supportive approach promotes better listening by both parties, and permits a climate where disagreement is not only acceptable, but invited.

Creating an Open Atmosphere (CONT)

❏ 3. Reflect equality, not superiority.

Managers who put too much emphasis on their position and power often create barriers between themselves and their employees. Managers who share information with employees and then seek their opinions create a feeling of equality.

Here is an example:

>**Superiority:** "I was doing it this way before you were born."

>**Equality:** "We have done it this way for years but I would like to hear your ideas on how we can do it better."

Employees appreciate a manager who shares information, asks for opinions, and listens to ideas. Managers who understand this have appraisal discussions that are more enlightening and productive.

❏ 4. Be accepting, not dogmatic.

Managers who approach decisions, plans, and problems dogmatically are telling employees there is no need for other ideas or solutions. Things have already been decided. This can demoralize an employee who has ideas and wants to excel. Managers who listen to employee input, or allow their ideas to be challenged in a search for the best solution, stimulate enthusiasm, creativity, and productivity. Here is an example that contrasts the two approaches:

>**Dogmatic:** "This is the best solution."

>**Accepting:** "This is the best solution I could come up with. What other possibilities do you see?"

A manager who accepts employees' input recognizes their value, capitalizes on their knowledge, and builds confidence in the group.

Appraisal Questions

Create an Exchange of Information

Effective appraisal questions can provide some very important benefits because:

- ▶ They require the manager's commitment to listen.

- ▶ They stimulate thought about specific issues.

- ▶ They solicit another person's ideas, point of view, and/or feelings.

- ▶ They provide an opportunity to test an idea against the reasoning of someone else.

- ▶ They elicit important information that might not otherwise be revealed. Employees like to talk to managers about their work, the organization, their ideas, and their accomplishments. Well-presented questions give them that opportunity, and everyone profits from the results.

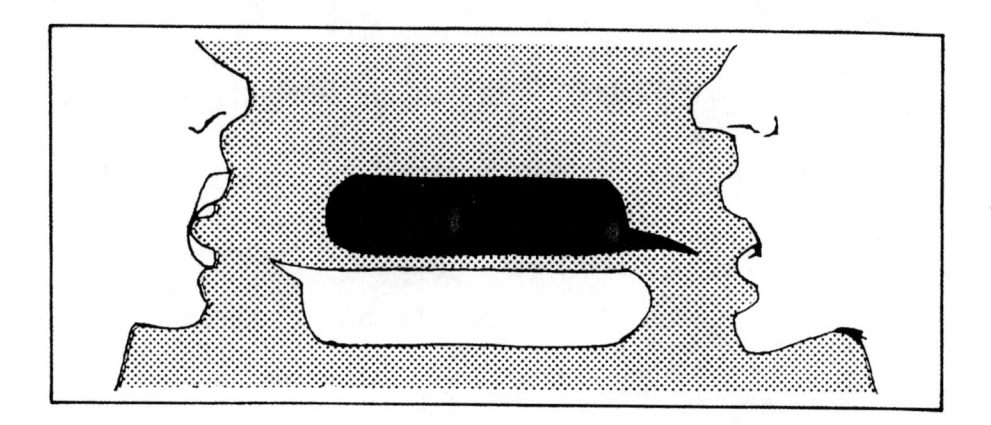

Appraisal Questions (CONT)

Facilitate the Discussion

There are three types of questions that can be used to help the manager and employee better understand each other's point of view:

- open-ended
- reflective
- directive

1. Open-Ended Questions

These are questions that cannot be answered with a yes or no. These questions require an opinion or expression of feelings.

For example:

"What is your opinion of...?"
"How do you feel about...?"
"What do you think caused...?"

Advantages of open-ended questions include:

- a demonstration of your interest in the other person's point of view
- a confirmation that you value the other person's ideas and feelings
- a stimulation of thought about specific issues
- a better understanding of the other person's needs
- the encouragement of a dialogue rather than a monologue

2. Reflective Questions

A reflective question repeats a statement the other person has made, in the form of a question. Good listening skills are required. It is also important to select the most significant feeling or idea stated.

For example:

>**Employee:** "Our results would be better if we modified the procedures used to take samples."
>
>**Manager:** "You're convinced the results can be improved?"

Reflective questions can be helpful because:

> ➤ Arguments can be avoided. You respond without accepting or rejecting what has been said.

> ➤ They confirm that you understand what has been said. If you reflect incorrectly, the other person has an opportunity to correct you.

> ➤ The other person is encouraged to clarify or expand upon what has been said.

> ➤ The other person can recognize illogical statements he or she might have made if the statement comes back in a nondirective fashion.

> ➤ They create a dialogue conducive to agreement.

Appraisal Questions (CONT)

3. Directive Questions

These are questions used to solicit information about a particular point or issue. Directive questions are usually reserved until after the other person has finished talking on the subject. Directive questions can then be used to sustain communication, or obtain information or ideas in which you are specifically interested.

For example:

> **Manager:** "If you are convinced the result can be improved, what steps would you take and when would you take them?"

Directive questions have these advantages:

- ▶ They provide pertinent information in those areas of greatest importance to you.

- ▶ They challenge the other person to explore ideas, defend statements, and contribute suggestions.

- ▶ They offer both parties specific facts on an issue.

Open-ended, reflective, and directive questions are all useful techniques to draw the employee into a thorough discussion of job performance and personal development.

The appraisal discussion is more than a simple review of job performance. It should progress naturally to a discussion of how the employee can do a better job in the future. It is also a good time to draw out the employee's ambitions and aspirations.

Personal Development and Growth

As performance is discussed, it often becomes apparent that additional training and development are required or desirable. It is also possible that the discussion will provide an indication that an employee is ready for more responsibility, which requires new or improved skills.

Therefore, specific areas for improvement and the need for new skill development should be discussed. Techniques by which further growth can be accomplished should also be covered. The manager should encourage the employee to talk about personal growth needs, so goals to meet them can be established. This effort can be supported by:

- ➤ serving as a sounding board to explore developmental alternatives
- ➤ testing the extent to which the employee has thought through developmental objectives
- ➤ providing a supportive climate for learning

The final employee development plans should be specific and include agreement by the employee for:

- ➤ what the employee needs to do
- ➤ when the employee needs to do it
- ➤ what the manager needs to do and when
- ➤ once development is completed, how it is to be applied

For more information on coaching, refer to <u>Coaching and Counseling</u>, Crisp Series.

The Importance of Attitude

The appraiser's attitude toward the appraisal discussion will make a genuine difference in the outcome. A well-led session provides an opportunity to share ideas and points of view, and to discuss problems and successes.

The manager who acts as though the appraisal process is an imposition, shows impatience with the employee's questions, and/or is skeptical of the employee's ability to accomplish his or her goals, will most likely do more to decrease morale and productivity than to lift it.

Likewise, the manager who is openly critical of the organization and the quality of upper management, and/or is skeptical of the organization's future will do more harm than good.

The manager who approaches the discussion with a positive attitude, reflects a genuine interest in the employee, and is open to personal feedback will usually find the employee receptive and the discussion stimulating.

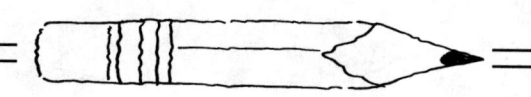

CHARACTERISTICS OF AN EFFECTIVE DISCUSSION LEADER

The following characteristics are essential to effective performance appraisal discussions. This scale will help you identify strengths and determine areas where improvement would be beneficial. Circle the number that best reflects where you fall on the scale; the higher the number, the more you are like the characteristic. When you have finished, total the numbers circled in the space provided below.

1. I let the employee do most of the talking.
   10   9   8   7   6   5   4   3   2   1

2. I make an intense effort to listen to the employee's ideas.
   10   9   8   7   6   5   4   3   2   1

3. I am prepared to suggest solutions to problems and developmental needs, but let the employee contribute first.
   10   9   8   7   6   5   4   3   2   1

4. My statements about performance are descriptive, not judgmental.
   10   9   8   7   6   5   4   3   2   1

5. I reinforce the positives in performance as well as seek ways to eliminate the negatives.
   10   9   8   7   6   5   4   3   2   1

6. I try to support the employee's ideas rather than force my own.
   10   9   8   7   6   5   4   3   2   1

7. I invite alternatives rather than assume there is only one way to approach an issue.
   10   9   8   7   6   5   4   3   2   1

8. I use open-ended, reflective, and directive questions to stimulate discussion.
   10   9   8   7   6   5   4   3   2   1

9. I am specific and descriptive when I express a concern about performance.
   10   9   8   7   6   5   4   3   2   1

10. My employees know I want them to succeed.
    10   9   8   7   6   5   4   3   2   1

TOTAL _____

WHERE ARE YOU?

A score between 90 and 100 indicates you should be leading successful discussions. Scores between 70 and 89 indicate significant strengths plus a few improvement needs. A score between 50 and 69 reflects some strength, but a significant number of problem areas as well. Scores below 50 call for a serious effort to improve in several categories. Make a special effort to grow in any area where you scored 6 or less regardless of your total score.

Achieving Third Base

You arrive at third base when both parties have had an opportunity to thoroughly discuss all aspects of performance during the appraisal period. Identify development needs and agree on a performance plan for the next period.

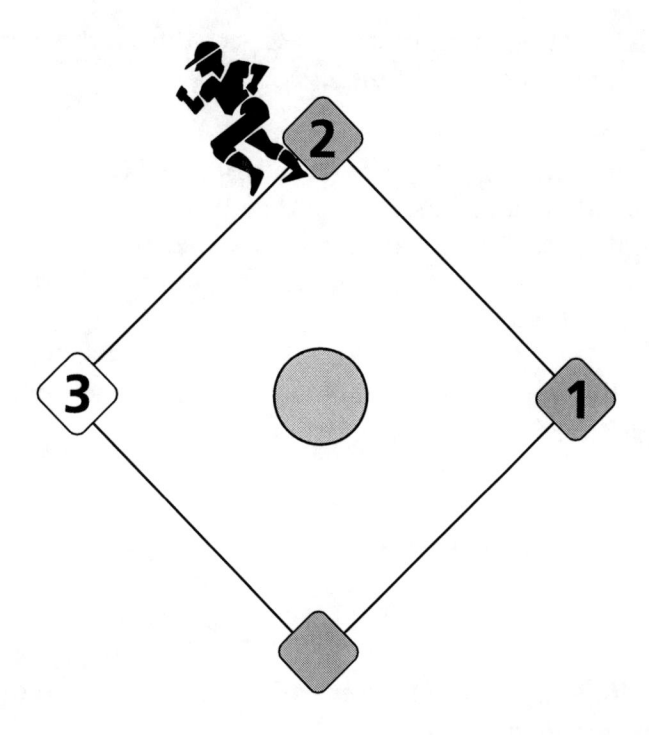

> **TIP:** Employee response to the appraisal may differ from what you expect. It is a good idea, therefore, to give some thought to the range of possible responses in advance, and make plans accordingly.

Closing the Appraisal Discussion

After the manager and employee have concluded discussion of past performance, addressed any development needs, and established new goals and/or standards for the future, they need to take time to review these agreements and plans. Many performance reviews fail because participants end the session with differing perceptions about what was accomplished and what was agreed.

To prevent miscommunication of what is expected from the employee, the manager should conclude the discussion by:

1 **Summarizing what has been discussed and agreed.** This should be done positively and enthusiastically. Be sure to include commitments you have made. If some areas of disagreement occurred, review how you and the employee have agreed they will be resolved.

2 **Giving the employee a chance to react**, question, and add additional ideas and suggestions

3 **Expressing appreciation** for the employee's participation and reinforcing the commitment to future plans

4 **Following the discussion with a written record** of the agreements and/or action plans

Note: As an alternative approach, the manager might find it worthwhile to have the employee summarize the discussion and prepare the written record of the agreements and/or action plans. This will give the employee more "ownership" of the outcomes and action plans, and the manager the chance to evaluate his or her reaction to the appraisal process.

For more information on feedback, refer to <u>Feedback Skills for Leaders</u>, *Crisp Series.*

Case Situations

After reading each example, indicate how you would react.

Situation 1:

The employee agrees with the appraisal and wants to improve. Some genuine differences of opinion are expressed, but the employee makes positive efforts to clarify the issues rather than be defensive.

Your response: _____

_____

_____

Situation 2:

The employee does not accept responsibility for his substandard performance and blames company politics and other employees.

Your response: _____

_____

Situation 3:

The employee disagrees with elements of your appraisal and offers specific information to refute your findings.

Your response: _____

_____

_____

Situation 4:

The employee accepts the appraisal without saying a word and prepares to leave before you have discussed the next performance plan.

Your response: _____

_____

Compare your responses with the author's in the back of the book.

PART 5

After the Appraisal

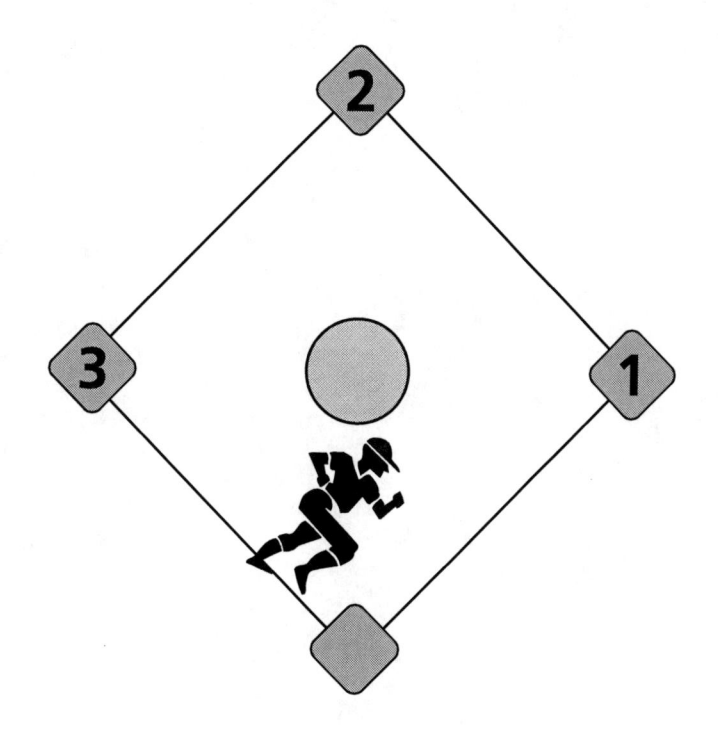

You Score a Home Run When a Post-Appraisal Analysis Reflects a Job Well Done by Both Parties

Following Up—Three Suggestions

1 Put It in Writing

Once the performance appraisal discussion has been concluded, the manager should see that a written record is made immediately. This may be done by either the manager or the employee and should include:

- a summary of the overall appraisal for the previous period
- plans to which both parties agreed
- any personal commitments the manager has made requiring specific action

Both the manager and the employee should have a copy of the written record.

2 Take Time to Reflect

Following each review is a good time to reflect on your performance in leading the discussion. Some questions to consider are:

- What was done well?
- What was done poorly?
- What was learned about the employee?
- What was learned about self and job? Did the employee give you any feedback that gave you some new insights about yourself?
- What will be done differently next time?

3 Always Follow Through

The third element of follow-up is to ensure that agreements are kept and plans followed. If this is not done, the entire appraisal loses its impact and the employee assumes no one cares very much about performance or commitments. This phase of the follow-up is actually the foundation for the next appraisal.

To review what you have read, and to plan your next performance appraisal, study the checklist on the next two pages.

Performance Appraisal Checklist for Managers

The following checklist is designed to guide the manager in preparing, conducting, and following through on employee performance appraisal discussions.

I. PERSONAL PREPARATION

- ❏ I have reviewed mutually-understood expectations with respect to job duties, projects, goals, standards, and any other predetermined performance factors pertinent to this appraisal discussion.

- ❏ I have observed job performance measured against mutually understood expectations. In so doing, I have done my best to avoid such pitfalls as:
  - Bias/prejudice
  - The vagaries of memory
  - Overattention to some aspects of the job at the expense of others
  - Being overly influenced by my own experience
  - Trait evaluation rather than performance measurement

- ❏ I have reviewed the employee's background, including:
  - Skills
  - Work experience
  - Training

- ❏ I have determined the employee's performance strengths and areas in need of improvement, and in so doing have:
  - Accumulated specific, unbiased documentation that can be used to help communicate my position
  - Limited myself to those critical points that are the most important
  - Prepared a possible development plan in case the employee needs assistance in coming up with a suitable plan

- ❏ I have identified areas for concentration in setting goals and standards for the next appraisal period.

- ❏ I have given the employee advance notice of when the discussion will be held, and have been clear on my expectations of what is to be covered so that he or she can prepare.

- ❏ I have set aside an adequate block of uninterrupted time to permit a full and complete discussion.

II. CONDUCTING THE APPRAISAL DISCUSSION

- ❏ I plan to begin the discussion by creating a sincere but open and friendly atmosphere. This includes:
  - Reviewing the purpose of the discussion
  - Making it clear that it is a joint discussion for the purpose of mutual problem-solving and goal-setting
  - Striving to put the employee at ease

- ❏ In the body of the discussion, I intend to keep the focus on job performance and related factors. This includes:
  - Discussing job requirements: employee strengths, accomplishments, improvement needs, and evaluating results of performance against objectives set during previous reviews and discussions
  - Being prepared to cite observations for each point I want to discuss
  - Encouraging the employee to appraise his or her own performance
  - Using open-ended, reflective, and directive questions to promote thought, understanding, and problem-solving

- ❏ I will encourage the employee to outline his or her personal plans for self-development before suggesting ideas of my own. In the process, I will:
  - Try to get the employee to set personal growth and improvement targets
  - Strive to reach agreement on appropriate development plans that detail what the employee intends to do and a timetable and support I am prepared to give

- ❏ I am prepared to discuss work assignments, projects, and goals for the next appraisal period, and will ask the employee to come prepared with his or her suggestions.

Performance Appraisal Checklist for Managers (CONT)

III. CLOSING THE DISCUSSION

❏ I will be prepared to make notes during the discussion for the purpose of summarizing agreements and follow-up. In closing, I will:
- Summarize what has been discussed
- Show enthusiasm for plans that have been made
- Give the employee an opportunity to make additional suggestions
- End on a positive, friendly, harmonious note

IV. POST-APPRAISAL FOLLOW-UP

❏ As soon as the discussion is over, I will record the plans made, the points requiring follow-up, and the commitments I made, and provide a copy for the employee.

❏ I will also evaluate how I handled the discussion. This will include:
- What I did well
- What I could have done better
- What I learned about the employee and his or her job
- What I learned about myself and my job

Creating a Personal Action Plan

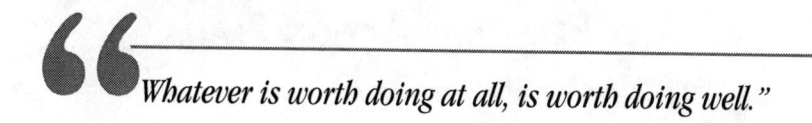

> *"Whatever is worth doing at all, is worth doing well."*
>
> –Philip Stanhope

Reflect for a moment on what you have been learning in this book, and contrast it with how you have done appraisals in the past. Have some new skills and behaviors that you need to learn and practice been presented? If so, you will need a personal action plan to focus your efforts and help assure you apply what you have learned.

A good way to get started is to think over the material in this book: the self-analysis questionnaires, the case studies, and the reinforcement exercises. What did you learn about performance appraisals? What did you learn about yourself? How can you apply what you learned?

Make a commitment to become better at performance appraisals.

My Personal Action Plan

1. My appraisal skills are strong in the following areas:

   _____
   _____
   _____

2. I need to improve the following appraisal skills:

   _____
   _____
   _____
   _____

3. My appraisal improvement goals are (be sure they are specific, attainable, and measurable):

   _____
   _____
   _____
   _____

4. Here are my action steps to accomplish my goals:

   _____
   _____
   _____

Name: _____
Date: _____

Author's Suggested Answers to Cases

Case Study 1—Who Will Be Better at Performance Appraisals?

With proper training and guidance, Janice and Arminio may both become excellent at performance appraisal. At this point, however, Janice has better instincts about how an appraisal should be approached. Employees need to know what is expected of them. When employees have an opportunity to participate in establishing goals and standards, they usually make good contributions and develop a strong sense of ownership. Contrary to Arminio's assumption, workers tend to set goals and standards too high rather than too low.

Case Study 2—What Upset Jess?

Jess may be upset because Darcy seems to have an attitude that reflects "I know best—what could you possibly contribute to this discussion of your performance?" Jess was asked to leave a meeting to come in for his appraisal discussion. This may have embarrassed him and he may have been seriously needed there. It does not appear the discussion had been scheduled in advance, so he had no opportunity to prepare. Darcy seems to think her time and her schedule are more important than anyone else's. Darcy's approach is: "Here's what's wrong and here's what to do about it." Jess has no opportunity for questions or input.

Author's Suggested Answers to Cases (cont)

Case Situations (from page 67)

Situation 1:

Express gratitude for the employee's active participation. This employee has voiced the expected response if you follow the process described in this book. Most employees want information about their strengths and weaknesses, and how to invest their time more profitably for improvement. Don't forget the importance of sincere praise when it is earned.

Situation 2:

Listen with an open mind. Without judging, interrupting, or arguing, try to find out why the person is placing the blame elsewhere. Then move the discussion toward corrective action that can be achieved with the employee's cooperation. Compliment the employee anytime a move is made toward accepting responsibility. Follow up closely and schedule another review soon to measure changes in the employee's point of view.

Situation 3:

Listen carefully to the employee, then indicate your willingness to re-examine your data. If the employee's information is more valid than yours is, modify your position accordingly. If you believe the employee's data is invalid or irrelevant, stand your ground and explain your position.

Situation 4:

Some individuals are intimidated by the appraisal process, and a special effort is required to open things up. Others may feel a quick agreement will save them from a discussion of their faults. When employees are reluctant to talk, encourage them by asking questions. Ask them to suggest activities that would help them. Ask them to summarize their performance. Ask for their conclusions at the end of the session. Ensure they provide input about their new performance plan.

Also Available

Books•Videos•Computer-Based Training Products

If you enjoyed this book, we have great news for you. There are over 200 books available in the *Crisp Fifty-Minute™ Series*. For more information visit us online at
www.axzopress.com

Subject Areas Include:

Management
Human Resources
Communication Skills
Personal Development
Sales/Marketing
Finance
Coaching and Mentoring
Customer Service/Quality
Small Business and Entrepreneurship
Training
Life Planning
Writing